THE HIGH-INCOME ENTREPRENEUR'S GUIDE
TO BUILDING A SUSTAINABLE BUSINESS
THAT PAYS YOU FOR LIFE

START, STAY AND BANK PROFITS™

NICOLE GILLYARD, CPA

Published by So It Is Written, LLC
Rochester, MI
SoItIsWritten.net

Start, Stay & Bank Profits™: The High-Income Entrepreneur's Guide to Building a Sustainable Business That Pays You for Life
Copyright © 2025 by Nicole Gillyard

Edited by: So It Is Written – www.SoItIsWritten.net

Formatting: Ya Ya Ya Creative – YaYaYaCreative@gmail.com

ISBN: 979-8-9993606-2-5

LCCN: 2025914884

PRINTED AND BOUND IN THE UNITED STATES OF AMERICA

TABLE OF CONTENTS

INTRODUCTION

———◇———

Somewhere along the journey to "success," many high-income entrepreneurs buy into a dangerous lie: *If you're making money, you must be doing fine.*

But here's the truth I've seen up close after working with thousands of business owners across the country as a CPA and business strategist: *Revenue is not the same as profit.* Profit alone doesn't guarantee peace, scalability, or legacy.

I've met six-figure earners who couldn't consistently pay themselves. I've reviewed tax returns for influencers with verified accounts and those who have struggled with financial stability. I've seen burned-out CEOs secretly hoping their next launch fails—just so they can finally rest.

You don't need to work *harder*. You need a better *system*. That's why I wrote *Start, Stay & Bank Profits*. This book is the blueprint for building a business that:

- Starts smart with the proper structure and pricing
- Stays solid with intentional operations and systems
- Banks profits that turn into *real* wealth—not just revenue

What Makes This Book Different?

This isn't a theory. The SSBP framework was built from the trenches—combining tax expertise, real-world coaching, and the operational strategies I use in my own businesses.

It's a practical, repeatable system designed for:

- Entrepreneurs who are making money, but feel stuck in the grind

- Professionals who want to build a business with structure, not stress

- Owners who want to *keep* what they earn and make money work for themselves

This isn't just about cash flow. It's about clarity, control, and capacity to build a business that works—with or without you.

How to Use This Book for Immediate Results

Each chapter is built around real decisions you must make: how to set up your business, how to pay yourself, how to manage your money, and how to plan for the future.

Here's how to get the most from it:

- **Don't just read. Do.** Each chapter includes prompts, examples, and a workbook section to apply what you learn right away.

- **Start where you are.** Whether you're launching, restructuring, or scaling, this book will meet you in your current season.

- **Commit to the process.** Profit isn't a moment. It's a mindset and a method. This book gives you both.

You've made the money. Now, let's help you *keep it, grow it, and finally enjoy it*—like the boss you are. Let's get to work!

—Nicole Gillyard, CPA
Founder of *Start, Stay & Bank Profits*™

Chapter 1

THE TRUTH ABOUT STARTING SMART

◇

Why Passion Isn't Enough & Profit Must Lead

*L*et me get right to it. Just because you're good at something doesn't mean it needs to be a business. That may sound harsh. But as a CPA who's reviewed thousands of financials and coached entrepreneurs across the country, I've seen far too many brilliant people turn their passion into poverty because they didn't start smart.

We've been sold a romantic idea that all you need is hustle, heart, and a website to become a successful business owner. But here's the truth most people won't say out loud:

It's not the *most passionate* entrepreneurs who succeed.
It's the most *prepared*.

Starting smart is about more than filing an LLC and getting a logo. It's about building the kind of business that pays you, not drains you. It's about structure, strategy, and sustainability. And, yes, it's about profit from day one.

The Fatal Mistake Most Entrepreneurs Make

When I sit across from new business owners and ask, "What's your profit model?" I usually get a confused look. They've got vision boards, Instagram handles, and maybe even a fancy Canva flyer. However, they have no idea how their business is actually going to generate revenue, cover expenses, and still pay them as the boss they claim to be.

They're building vibes, not value. And it's costing them time, energy, and money they'll never get back. If you want to stop playing business and start building wealth, you've got to understand what you're walking into.

This Chapter Will Help You:

- Evaluate whether your current or future business idea is actually bankable

- Choose a business model that aligns with profitability *and* your lifestyle

- Avoid common startup traps that leave entrepreneurs broke and burnt out

Let's start with the question most people avoid...

Is Your Business Idea Bankable?

Before you invest another dime, ask yourself:

1. **Is there a proven demand?**

    Not "Do I like this idea?" but "Are people already paying for this solution?" If you can't find competitors, that's not always a good thing. It might mean there's no market.

2. **Can you charge a premium?**

    Is your offer a *want* or a *need*? Businesses that solve urgent, painful problems are able to charge more, sell faster, and sustain longer.

3. **Does this model scale beyond you?**

    If your business requires you to work 80 hours a week just to survive, it's not a business. It's a job you created for yourself (without benefits).

    If you answered, "No" to any of those questions, I'm not saying shut it down. However, you do need to slow down and fix your foundation.

Choose a Model That Pays You — Not Just Feeds Your Ego

There are six core business models I see succeed consistently:

1. **Service-Based Consulting (High-Ticket)**

Low overhead, high margin, scalable with systems and subcontractors.

2. **Digital Products or Courses**

   Once built, it can scale infinitely. You trade knowledge for volume.

3. **Subscription or Membership**

   Recurring revenue = stability. Great for content creators or niche experts.

4. **Brick-and-Mortar (With Caution)**

   Only if the demand is proven *and* the margins make sense. Rent is real.

5. **Hybrid Models**

   Many of my clients have multiple income streams, but *one core offer* that runs the show.

6. **Licensing or Certification Programs**

   Turning your method into an asset others pay to use? That's next-level.

Bankable Doesn't Mean Boring

Let's kill the myth that innovative businesses are soulless. Structure doesn't cancel creativity. In fact, the more precise your business model, the *more* freedom you have to innovate.

I want your business to be beautiful *and* bankable. Aligned with your values, yes. But not allergic to profitability.

The Seven (7) Bankable Questions Every Founder Must Answer

Before you go further, answer these in your journal or workbook:

1. What *problem* does my business solve?

2. Who is *already* paying for this solution?

3. What makes my solution different or better?

4. What is the *price point* at which I can earn a healthy profit?

5. What *structure* (LLC, S-Corp, etc.) supports my financial goals?

6. What are my *monthly revenue* and *owner pay* targets?

7. What would make this business worth running — even when I don't feel like it?

In Case You're Thinking, "I Already Started Wrong..."

Listen, it's never too late to refine your structure, increase your prices, and reposition your business for genuine wealth. This chapter isn't about shame. It's about clarity.

You have the power to reboot, restructure, and reposition. You just need the right framework.

And that's precisely what we're doing here. You're laying the foundation so you don't build a business that breaks you.

Action Steps

- Write your current (or future) business model in three clear sentences.

- Identify where your pricing may not support long-term profitability.

- Book a call with your CPA (yes, like me) and review your entity + tax plan.

- Complete the *Bankable Business Scorecard* in your workbook.

Next up? We're delving deeper into legal structure and compliance as you build a business that can secure funding, pass due diligence, and pay you like a real CEO. Let's go fix the foundation — and make sure it can hold wealth.

Chapter 2

LEGAL, LEAN &
LAUNCH-READY

◇

How to Set Up a Business That's Compliant, Fundable, and Built to Bank

*L*et me save you from a painful lesson I've seen too many entrepreneurs learn the hard way: *If your business isn't set up right from Day 1, you will pay for it later — in taxes, lawsuits, or missed opportunities.*

I don't care how great your marketing is, how many clients you have, or how much your sales pop. If your structure is messy, your books are sloppy. Your legal foundation is cracked, and your business is at risk.

And let's be clear: *I'm not here to scare you. I'm here to get you ready.*

Why Getting "Legal" Isn't Optional

Many people skip the setup phase because they think it's too complicated or they're just "testing the waters." But what you're really doing is building on quicksand.

If you ever want to:

- Get funding or grants
- Bring on partners or team members
- Apply for contracts or licenses
- Protect your personal assets
- Avoid IRS headaches

You need to get your business *legit and lean.*

Let's walk through what that means.

First: Choose the Right Entity Structure

Here's the truth. Your business structure is one of the *most important tax decisions* you'll ever make. Don't just check a box or take a guess. Making the right choice can save you thousands of dollars each year.

Here's a simplified breakdown of your top options:

Entity Type	Best For	Tax Treatment	Risks/Notes
Sole Proprietor	Testing idea	Personal taxes only	High liability, no separation
LLC	Flexibility	Pass-through	Great first step, but consider tax election
S Corporation	Growing biz	Salary + distribution (tax savings!)	Must run payroll, more formal
C Corporation	Scaling, big profit	Corporate tax + potential double tax	Great for benefits, reinvestment, legacy planning
Nonprofit	Mission-driven orgs	Tax-exempt with IRS approval	Strict rules, needs board, no personal profit

CPA Tip: If your business is registered as an SP or LLC, and earns more than $50K net profit a year, talk to a CPA about electing *S Corp or C Corp* status. You'll thank me later.

Second: Get These Legal & Financial Ducks in a Row

Here's your Launch-Ready Checklist — no skipping steps:

- Register your business with your state. You can be registered in a home state and be a foreign entity in another state where your business functions or has an office.

- Apply for your EIN (free from the IRS at www.irs.gov/EIN).

- Open a separate business bank account, obtain a certificate of registration, and request an EIN letter.

- Set up your accounting system, preferably one that links to your bank accounts.

- Choose a business address (even a virtual one is better than your home).

- Draft basic contracts and service agreements.* I recommend hiring a professional business attorney or,

---

* Contracts and service agreements further discussed in Chapter 4, Build the Back-Office First

at minimum, have your contracts reviewed by an attorney before finalizing.

- Get business insurance (liability, cyber, and errors & omissions, if applicable).

- File any licenses or permits required in your industry or city of operation.

If you can't check these boxes yet, *pause the hustle* and handle this first.

Why Fundability Matters

If your business is not structured to look legit on paper, you're going to get denied for loans, lines of credit, and even grants. Lenders and investors look for:

- Business accounts and financials and to make sure they are separate from personal accounts

- Proper EIN and tax filings

- Consistency across documents (name, address, bank, entity type)

- Monthly or quarterly revenue reports

- Contracts and systems in place

You're not just setting up a business. You're building an *asset* that others can trust, back, and support.

Common Mistakes That Cost Entrepreneurs BIG

Let me give you some real-world CPA confessions — and they're all avoidable:

- Using your personal account for business income, then crying during tax season

- Setting up an LLC, but never electing S Corp status, missing out on $10K+ in tax savings

- Getting sued because you had no contract in place

- Hiring your cousin with no 1099 or payroll system — and now the IRS is knocking

- Applying for grants with inconsistent business info and getting denied

You can do better. Now you know how.

Your Lean Back-Office Setup

A profitable business isn't just about front-end sales. It's about *back-end structure*.

Here's a lean setup you can build in one week:

Tech Stack:

- Bookkeeping: QuickBooks or Wave

- Invoicing: Stripe, PayPal Business, or Square

- Contracts: HelloSign, Dubsado, or Honeybook

- Banking: Novo, Bluevine, or a business account at your local bank or credit union

People:

- A CPA or tax pro you trust (not just at tax time)

- A virtual assistant or bookkeeper for admin

- An on-call business attorney (many offer low-cost consultations)

Documents:

- Operating agreement or bylaws

- Templates for client contracts

- SOPs for key tasks (sales, client onboarding, fulfillment)

Action Steps

1. Reevaluate your current business structure. Are you set up for tax efficiency?

2. Open separate business bank accounts, if you haven't already.

3. Get a meeting with a CPA (ahem ... me or someone like me).

4. Complete your *Launch-Ready Checklist* in the workbook.

5. Write down three "back office" gaps that could cost you and commit to fixing them this month.

Remember

Starting legally and lean isn't just smart. It's liberating. When your structure is correct, your confidence increases, your risk decreases, and your profits? They finally start making sense. Let's move forward and build on solid ground.

Chapter 2 Workbook includes:

- Entity comparison matrix

- Launch Ready checklist

- CPA prep questions

Chapter 3
PRICE LIKE A PRO
◇

Psychology and Math Behind Profitable Pricing

*J*f you're guessing at your prices or copying what the person next to you charges, I've got news for you: *you're probably not charging enough*. And you're not alone.

I've worked with six-figure earners who still can't explain where their price came from. They just "felt" like it was the right number. But vibes don't pay bills, and feelings don't fund freedom.

If you want to *bank profits*, you've got to price from *strategy*, not struggle. That means understanding your costs, your value, and your market — then owning your number like a CEO.

Let's Be Real: Why Most Entrepreneurs Undercharge

You want to be accessible. You don't want to hear, "That's too expensive." You don't want to scare people off.

But here's what's really happening:

- You're afraid to ask for more because you haven't built the confidence to back your offer.

- You're anchoring your prices to broke clients, not bold outcomes.

- You're stuck in survival mode, so you take whatever's offered to keep money flowing.

Let me stop you right there. Undercharging is not humble. It's harmful. It hurts your sustainability. It attracts the wrong clients. And it limits your ability to grow.

Let me share a true story that I utilize when teaching:

This is Widgets, LLC, a single-member LLC owned and operated by "Ruth." Ruth determined her costs to manufacture and sell her products and followed the pricing strategy below:

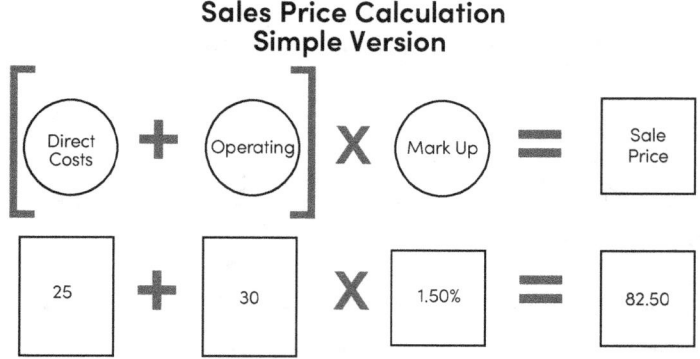

**Sales Price Calculation
Simple Version**

Scenario 1

At a selling price of $83 per widget, she not only covers every cost, but also earns a healthy profit. In Scenario 1, by moving 5,000 widgets at that price, her total revenue comes to $415,000. After subtracting both the direct cost of goods sold and operating expenses per unit, as outlined in the process, she arrives at a $140,000 profit.

Scenario 1		
Revenue (Sales price x Quantity) 83 x 5000	415,000.00	
Cost of Sales Direct Costs 25 x 5000 sold	125,000.00	Margin 70%
Gross Profit Margin	290,000.00	
Expenses Operating Costs 30 x 5000	150,000.00	
Net Income (Loss)	140,000.00	

Scenario 2

Suppose Ruth offers a referral discount to a family-friend client, dropping her widget price to $55 in hopes of winning more business. Although the selling price has fallen, her direct and overhead costs remain unchanged. So, instead of turning a profit, she ends up breaking-even at a 55% profit margin.

Scenario 2		
Revenue (Sales price x Quantity) 55 x 5000	275,000.00	
Cost of Sales Direct Costs 25 x 5000 sold	125,000.00	Margin 55%
Gross Profit Margin	150,000.00	
Expenses Operating Costs 30 x 5000	150,000.00	Break-even
Net Income (Loss)	–	

Scenario 3

Suppose Ruth, in her first year, has no clue about her costs and decides to charge $45 per widget in hopes of winning more business. Although the selling price appears substantial, grossing six figures, her direct and overhead costs remain unchanged. So, instead of turning a profit, she ends up with a ($50k) loss of 44% profit margin.

Scenario 3		
Revenue (Sales price x Quantity) 45 x 5000	225,000.00	
Cost of Sales Direct Costs 25 x 5000 sold	125,000.00	Margin 44%
Gross Profit Margin	100,000.00	
Expenses Operating Costs 30 x 5000	150,000.00	
Net Income (Loss)	(50,000.00)	

Step 1: Understand the Numbers Behind Your Price

Based on what we discussed in Scenarios 1-3, before we touch on value or strategy, let's get down to math.

Your Price Must Cover:

- Direct costs (tools, time, delivery)

- Overhead (admin, subscriptions, payroll, rent)

- Taxes (plan for 25–30% of profit)

- Profit (yes, this is separate from your salary!)

- Your salary (non-negotiable)

CPA Tip: Every dollar you charge should give you *at least a 30–50% margin after expenses*. Otherwise, you're working just to stay busy. The goal is to increase margin without impacting the quality of your product or service.

Terminology Note: Margin refers to the revenue available after covering direct costs to produce a product or provide services. The amount available must cover your overhead, taxes, profit, and owner compensation.

Step 2: Add the Value Multiplier

Now that you know what you *need*, let's build on what it's *worth*. Ask yourself:

- What problem does my offer solve?

- How urgent and painful is that problem?

- What's the financial or emotional cost of inaction?

- What does success look like for the client?

If your service helps someone make money, save time, reduce risk, or gain peace, it's worth more than you think. *Example:* If you help a business owner recover $10,000 in missed deductions, your price better not be $297.

Step 3: Choose a Pricing Model That Protects Your Energy

Here are four proven pricing structures that work:

Model	Best For	Warning
Hourly	Projects with unpredictable scope	Encourages trading time for money
Flat Rate / Package	Clear deliverables, fixed outcomes	Must calculate true cost & time accurately
Retainer	Ongoing support & advisory	Requires solid scope + boundaries
Value-Based	High-value transformation offers	Requires bold confidence + clear ROI

CPA Tip: My favorite? *Flat rate + results-focused.* That way, clients know what they're getting, and you know what you're being paid without micromanaging hours.

Step 4: Build Profit Into Your Price (Non-Negotiable)

Here's where I pull rank as your CPA and coach. You *must* bake profit into your pricing. If your price only covers costs, you are not profitable. You're just afloat. Set a rule: *No offer gets released until it includes a profit margin.*

If you're afraid clients won't pay, you either:

- Need to fix your messaging

- Need to shift your audience

- Need to deliver stronger outcomes

What you do is valuable. Stop pricing like you're a hobbyist.

Action Steps

1. Calculate the *true cost* to deliver your offer.

2. Set a *profit margin* goal (start at 30%).

3. Choose your *pricing model* (hourly, flat, retainer, value-based).

4. Create a *pricing sheet* with confidence and stop hiding your rates.

5. Complete the *Profitable Pricing Calculator* in your workbook.

Coming up next: We'll move into Chapter 4 and set up your business systems and back office so you're not just charging right, but *collecting* right.

Chapter 4

BUILD THE
BACK OFFICE FIRST

◇

Create the Financial Systems
That Keep Your Business Legal,
Bankable, and Scalable

*I*f your business can't run without you chasing paperwork, texting contractors at midnight, or digging through emails to find your last invoice, you don't have a business. You have chaos wearing a cute logo. Let's fix that.

Too many entrepreneurs prioritize branding, social media, and sales pages, but overlook the aspects that actually make their business sustainable: the back office. I'm talking about your financial systems, standard operating procedures, and admin operations that keep the engine running even when you're not in the driver's seat.

You cannot scale mess.

You cannot fund chaos.

And you definitely can't *bank profits* from a business that has no infrastructure.

So, I need you to hear me as both your CPA and your strategist. *Before you market your next offer, get your back office right.*

What Is the Back Office Really?

Your back office is every part of your business that no one sees, but everyone *feels*.

It includes:

- How you receive and track money (invoicing, accounting, tax setup)

- How you deliver your services (workflow, automation, templates)

- How your team communicates and executes (file storage, meetings, SOPs)

- How you manage legal and financial compliance (contracts, insurance, licenses)

This is the "under the hood" part of the business. It's where most small businesses lose their money, time, and sanity.

The Consequences of a Messy Back Office

Let me break it down because I've seen it all:

- *Unpaid invoices* because you forgot to follow up

- *Tax debt* because you didn't set aside what you owed

- *Missed opportunities* because your business couldn't pass basic due diligence

- *Lawsuits* because you had no contracts or insurance

- *Burnout* because everything runs through you

And here's the real cost. When your business isn't built to run without you, you can't rest, sell, or step away. That's not freedom. That's a fancy cage.

Why You Must Be Bankable

Let's talk money. If you want:

- A business loan

- A line of credit

- A grant

- To get acquired

- To license your method

- To impress an investor

...they're not just looking at your Instagram. They're looking at your paperwork. Can you show twelve months of clean financial statements? Do your legal documents match your business name and address? Can you produce a profit & loss statement in twenty-four hours? That's what bankable means. And it starts with your back office.

Set Up These Core Financial Systems

1. **Business Bank Accounts (at least 3):**
   — Operating (for everyday business expenses)

   — Tax Holding (set aside 25–30% of profit)

   — Profit Reserve (emergency funds, expansion, or owner bonuses)

2. **Bookkeeping Software:**
   — QuickBooks, Xero, or Wave (find the accounting app that suites you)

   — Sync to bank accounts and update *weekly*

   — Categorize income and expenses properly

   — Generate P&L and balance sheet monthly

3. **Invoicing + Payment Collection:**
   — Use Stripe, Square, or HoneyBook

   — Send contracts *before* services begin

   — Automate reminders for overdue invoices

4. **Document Storage & Naming System:**
   — Google Drive or Dropbox with folders for Finance, Legal, Clients, Marketing

— Use naming formats like 2025_ClientAgreement_Johnson

— Store signed contracts, W9s, EIN letters, and licenses in one secure location

---

SOPs: Your Secret Weapon

Standard Operating Procedures (SOPs) are the difference between you being a solo hustler and a real CEO.

Ask yourself:

- If you stepped away for thirty days, could someone else onboard a client on your behalf?

- Would they know how to invoice, respond to a refund request, or post a blog?

- Would they have access to passwords, tools, and workflows?

If the answer is, "No," you don't have SOPs. You have mental notes. And that's not scalable. Start with documenting your top five processes:

1. Client onboarding

2. Payment & invoicing

3. Refund policy & response

4. Delivering your signature service

5. Weekly or monthly CEO check-in

Write them like you're teaching a bright fifteen-year-old how to run your business.

Clean Up Your Contracts

You don't need a $10K lawyer on retainer, but you *do* need:

- A standard service agreement (scope, timeline, payment terms)

- A confidentiality clause (especially for coaching or consulting)

- A clear cancellation and refund policy

- Contracts with every 1099 contractor (and a W9 from them, too)

- A working knowledge of how to enforce a contract (and when to walk away)

CPA Tip: Make your contracts easy to read, not stuffed with legalese that *you* don't understand.

Audit Yourself: Are You Really Set Up?

Here's a quick self-check:

System	In Place	Needs Work
Separate business bank account		
Tax savings system (account or %)		
Bookkeeping software connected		
SOPs written for key workflows		
Client & contractor contracts		
Organized digital file system		

If more than two boxes are empty or "need work," pause your hustle and fix the foundation.

Action Steps: Build Your Back Office Like a Boss

1. Set up or review three bank accounts: operations, taxes, and profit.

2. Schedule a weekly "Money Monday" to update books and review accounts.

3. Document your five most frequent tasks or processes.

4. Review your contracts for clarity, compliance, and client protection.

5. Organize your digital files and back them up in the cloud.

Final Word:
Your Business Deserves Structure

You are not too small for structure. You are not too early for systems. You are not too broke for boundaries. The back office is where wealth protection starts. It's how your business earns trust. And it's how you go from survival to scale. Build the back office before you build anything else.

Chapter 5
DON'T JUST WORK
— OPERATE

◇

Step Into Your CEO Seat with Structure and Systems

*L*et's be honest. Most entrepreneurs didn't start a business. They built themselves a job. They're hustling every day, responding to DMs, handling clients, making sales, sending invoices, and doing *everything* themselves. And while it might look successful from the outside, inside, it feels like a state of panic. If that's you, I need you to hear this: *You are not just a service provider. You are the* CEO.

And CEOs don't spend their days putting out fires. CEOs build systems. They monitor performance. They make strategic decisions and protect the business's ability to grow. This chapter discusses how to transition from performing the work to managing *the operation*.

Stop Being the Hustler — Start Being the Operator

You cannot scale what you can't see. And if everything lives in your head, your inbox, or a spiral notebook … your business is fragile. Let me say it another way: If you got sick for two weeks, and your business would collapse, *you don't have a business—you have a dependency.* We're changing that.

CEO Moves vs. Worker Bee Habits

Most founders start with worker bee habits and never outgrow them. That's why burnout is so high, especially for high achievers like you.

Let's compare:

Worker Bee	CEO
Chases tasks all-day	Prioritizes outcomes
Operates from urgency	Operates from vision
Says yes to everything	Protects their time
Reacts to problems	Builds preventative systems
Micromanages team	Delegates with clarity

If you want CEO-level results, you need CEO-level habits.

What It Really Means to Operate

To "operate" is to manage your business as an asset, not just a hustle. It means:

- Having *weekly rhythms* that keep things flowing

- Knowing your *key performance indicators (KPIs)*

- Creating *systems for marketing, sales, delivery, and admin*

- *Delegating* based on data, not desperation

- Building a *culture*, even if your team is small

You don't need a huge organizational chart to run like a CEO. You need clarity, commitment, and calendar control.

Your Weekly CEO Structure

I teach my clients a method I call the CEO Operating Week. It brings order to your chaos and protects your highest-value time. Here's how to structure it:

- **Money Monday**
  — Review financials (revenue, expenses, owner pay).

  — Check cash flow, invoices, and tax reserves.

  — Make profit allocations.

- **Team Tuesday**
  — Delegate tasks.

  — Review progress with VAs or contractors.

  — Clarify expectations.

- **Workflow Wednesday**

— Audit systems (including emails, content, and automation).

— Document or refine an SOP.

— Review client deliverables.

- **Thinking Thursday**

— Do the deep work of content creation, product development, visioning.

— Set strategic priorities.

— Dream and plan, not just execute.

- **Freedom Friday**

— Half-day or full-day off

— CEO check-in: What worked well this week and what didn't?

— Rest or invest in your own growth.

If you follow this rhythm for even ninety days, your business will feel different — lighter, clearer, and way more strategic.

Know Your KPIs Like a CEO

CEOs don't manage vibes. They manage *data*. That doesn't mean you need a complicated dashboard. Just track what matters:

Area	Key Metric
Revenue	Weekly and monthly income
Operations	% of tasks delegated
Marketing	Leads generated or content published
Sales	Conversion rate
Client Work	# of active clients or success rate
Time	Hours worked per week

Track them weekly or biweekly. Use your data to decide what gets attention and what gets cut.

Time Blocking = Power

One of the most significant CEO power moves is time blocking. If your calendar isn't protecting your priorities, someone else's agenda will run your life.

Block time for:

- Deep work (no calls or emails)

- Sales and follow-ups

- Content and visibility

- Financial review

- Breaks and personal time

CEO Tip: If it's not on your calendar, it's not a priority. It's a wish.

Document and Delegate

If it's repeatable, it should be documented. If it's documented, it can be delegated. And if it can be delegated, you can grow.

Start with:

- Your email process

- Client onboarding

- Social media posting

- Billing and follow-up

- Scheduling calls

Use Loom, Google Docs, or templates. You don't need to be fancy. You just need to be clear.

Start Operating Like a Boss

Let's recap what it looks like to *operate*:

- Weekly CEO structure

- Time blocked for revenue + strategy

- KPIs tracked and reviewed

- SOPs documented

- Delegation strategy in place

- Space to think, plan, and lead

Action Steps:
Step Into the Operator's Seat

1. Build your CEO Operating Week using the model above.

2. Choose three KPIs to track weekly.

3. Identify two tasks you can delegate or automate this month.

4. Block out CEO time in your calendar and *protect* it.

5. Start a simple SOP folder with at least three documented processes.

Final Word: Stop Just Doing — Start Deciding.

You're not here to stay busy. You're here to build something that works *without burning you out*. You are the boss. You are the asset. You are the architect of your future. And it's time your calendar, your systems, and your habits reflected that. Let's operate.

Chapter 6
KNOW YOUR NUMBERS
(or Die Slowly)

◇

Make Powerful Financial Decisions with Clarity and Control

*T*here's no way around it. If you don't know your numbers, you don't know your business. I've seen entrepreneurs bring in $30,000 a month and still feel broke. Why? Because money came in, but it flew right back out. No clarity. No system. No control.

They were running a "six-figure" brand and couldn't afford to pay themselves. Here's the hard truth: *hustle is not a substitute for financial literacy.* If you're serious about building a profitable business, you need to become fluent in your numbers—not just at tax time—but year round.

Why Entrepreneurs Avoid the Numbers (and What It's Costing You)

Let's call it out:

- You're scared of what the numbers will reveal.

- You think you're "not a numbers person".

- You've been winging it and haven't gotten burned yet.

- You confuse money *in* the account with actual profit.

But what you avoid is where the leak lives. Avoiding your numbers leads to the following:

- Surprise tax bills

- Overspending

- Underpricing

- Missed growth opportunities

- Paycheck-to-paycheck cycles, even with high revenue

You need to stop hoping things work out and start managing like a real CEO.

Three Financial Reports You Must Know

You don't need a degree in accounting. But you do need to know how to read and use these three:

1. **Profit & Loss Statement (P&L)**
   - Shows your income and expenses over time
   - Reveals whether you're actually making money

Key items:
- Gross revenue
- Cost of goods sold (COGS)

- Gross profit

- Operating expenses

- Net income (AKA profit)

Review this monthly. It tells you the *story* of your business.

2. **Cash Flow Statement**
    - Tracks money in vs. money out

    - Indicates whether your business is financially stable and can meet its obligations

Profit ≠ cash. You can be "profitable" on paper and still be broke if your cash is tied up in unpaid invoices, debt, or delayed launches. Use this to avoid overdrafts, missed payroll, or poor timing.

3. **Balance Sheet**
    - Snapshot of what your business owns vs. owes

    - Lists your assets, liabilities, and equity

This is what banks, grantors, and investors want to see. It shows how "healthy" your business really is, not just what you're earning.

Track These KPIs Like a CEO

Every business owner should be tracking at least these five metrics each month:

Metric	Why It Matters
Revenue	Shows sales growth or decline
Expenses	Reveals spending habits and areas to reduce
Net Profit	Actual money left after all expenses
Owner Pay	Are you paying yourself consistently and fairly?
Tax Withholding	Avoids surprise IRS bills — set aside 25–30% of profit

Optional:

- Customer Acquisition Cost (CAC)

- Client Lifetime Value (LTV)

- Gross Margin %

You don't need a huge dashboard. A simple spreadsheet cr weekly summary works fine.

Understanding the Difference: Cash Flow vs. Profit

This one often trips up many founders.

- *Profit* is what's left after all expenses (on paper).

- *Cash flow* refers to the actual movement of money in and out of an entity.

Let's say you close a $15K contract in January, but the client pays you in three installments. Your P&L shows the full $15K, but your bank account doesn't have it yet. This is why managing cash flow is key to staying alive.

Set Up a Simple Review System

Here's what a healthy monthly routine looks like:

Week 1 (Money Monday):

- Review the previous month's P&L.

- Check current account balances.

- Categorize uncategorized expenses.

Week 2:

- Update the KPI tracker.

- Follow up on unpaid invoices.

- Check tax set-aside and profit accounts.

Week 3–4:

- Analyze trends (spending, income dips, client churn).

- Prepare for significant expenses or launches.

- Meet with your bookkeeper or review reports.

CPA Tip: Don't wait until the end of the year. Financial health is a *monthly habit*, not a year-end panic.

Make Better Decisions With Better Data

When you know your numbers:

- You price confidently.

- You hire smarter.

- You plan for taxes early.

- You pay yourself on time.

- You attract lenders, buyers, and partners who trust your structure.

It's not just about compliance. It's about *control*. You'll stop asking, "Can I afford this?" and start deciding, "Do I want this based on strategy?"

Action Steps: Become a Financially Literate CEO

1. Choose a bookkeeping tool (QuickBooks, Wave, Xero) and commit to using it.

2. Schedule a monthly "Money CEO Day."

3. Track your five core metrics: revenue, expenses, profit, owner pay, and tax set-aside.

4. Meet with your accountant at least quarterly.

5. Review your P&L, Balance Sheet, and Cash Flow every month.

Final Word: Don't Die Broke With a Pretty Brand

Your Canva looks cute. Your website is stunning. But if your numbers are a mess, you're building a brand with no backbone. I don't care how "creative" or "visionary" you are. If you want to stay in business, you must know your numbers.

You deserve to make money and *keep* it. You deserve to feel confident when tax season rolls around. You deserve to look at your bank account and see the truth, not a lie. Numbers don't lie. And when you know them, you won't have to either. Let's go from guessing to governing, one Money Monday at a time.

Chapter 7

HIRE FOR PROFIT, NOT POPULARITY

◇

Build a Lean, High-Performance Team That Supports Your Bottom Line

*I*f your team is costing more than they're contributing, it's not a team. It's a payroll problem. Hiring is one of the most emotional and expensive moves a business owner can make. And too many people get it wrong.

- They hire too fast, with no clarity on ROI.

- They hold on to the wrong people out of guilt.

- They think more bodies mean more business.

But let me tell you the truth: *more people doesn't mean more profit*. Hiring is a growth tool, not a validation move. It's about *roles*, not *relationships*. And if you do it right, it will free your time, multiply your revenue, and strengthen your brand.

The First Rule of Hiring: You Hire for a Result, Not a Role

Don't just hire a "VA" or "Admin Assistant" because everyone says you need one. That's vague, and it invites wasted time. Instead, ask:

- *What specific outcome am I hiring for?*

- *What revenue or capacity will this person create or protect?*

- *How will I measure if they're doing a good job?*

For example: "I'm hiring a VA to take over client onboarding and calendar management so I can focus on sales calls and visibility." Now we're clear. That's a profit-aligned hire.

When Should You Hire?

You're spending ten or more hours a week on tasks that don't require *your* brain. You have documented systems in place for what needs to be done. You can clearly define a 30–60–90 day success plan. The role will either generate revenue or free you up to do so.

You're overwhelmed, but unclear. You don't have time to train. You think hiring will "fix" broken systems. You haven't run your numbers.

CPA Tip: If hiring someone costs $2,000 per month, you need a plan to earn $ 4,000 or more from the time or function they free up.

The Profit-Driven Hiring Formula

Let's do some math. If your average hourly value is $250/hour (based on revenue divided by hours worked), but you're spending ten hours/week doing admin work:

- That's $2,500 per week in value being wasted.

- That's $10,000 per month you're losing to busyness.

Now, imagine paying someone $25 per hour to take over those tasks. That's $1,000 per month to save $10,000 in lost opportunity. That's the power of a profitable hire.

Document Before You Delegate

Hiring without SOPs is setting your money on fire.

Before you post a job:
- Write out the task step-by-step.

- Create a Loom video or screen recording.

- Organize access to the tools they'll need.

- Define KPIs for the position.

Think like a franchisor. Could someone replicate this process without needing you to explain it live?

How to Keep the Right People

Good hires deserve good leadership. Protect your profit by leading well:

- Hold weekly or biweekly check-ins.

- Set clear boundaries (hours, response time, channels).

- Give feedback early and often.

- Reward performance, not presence.

You don't need a family. You need a functional team.

Action Steps:
Hire Like a CEO, Not a Hustler

1. Identify three tasks you can delegate profitably.

2. Calculate your hourly value.

3. Document one SOP this week.

4. Create a simple role description and test project.

5. Choose to hire slow and lead smart.

Final Word: Lean Teams, Strong Profits

A team should increase your capacity, reduce your stress, and expand your profits. If it's not doing that, something is broken. It's your job to fix it. Stop hiring because you're tired. Start hiring because you're ready to grow.

Chapter 8
RETENTION IS REVENUE

———◇———

Create Sticky Offers, High-Lifetime Value Clients, and Recurring Income

*W*ant to know the most overlooked growth strategy in small business?

Client retention.

It costs five to seven times more to acquire a new customer than to retain an existing one. But what do most entrepreneurs do? They chase new leads constantly while their past clients walk out the back door.

Let me make it plain: *Your most profitable offer is the one that keeps people coming back.*

———

Why Clients Leave — and How to Stop It

Clients don't leave because of price. They leave because of:

- Lack of communication
- Inconsistent delivery

- No clear next step

- No emotional connection

- No perceived progress

Retention isn't about trickery. It's about *trust* and *transformation*.

The Retention Flywheel

Here's how to build a business that keeps clients coming back and referring others.

1. **Strong Onboarding**

   First impressions matter. A great onboarding experience includes:

   - Welcome email or video

   - Clear instructions and timelines

   - Access to tools or community

   - What to expect next

This sets the tone and reduces the likelihood of refund requests or confusion.

2. **Consistent Communication**

   Clients don't want silence. Build regular touchpoints:
   - Weekly check-ins or progress reports

- Office hours or Q&A

- Monthly review calls

Staying in touch increases perceived value.

3. **Surprise and Delight**

   Add unexpected value:

   - Bonus resources or tools

   - Milestone celebrations

   - Handwritten thank-yous

   - Exclusive discounts or gifts

Small surprises build big loyalty.

4. *Next-Level Offers*

   Don't leave clients at the finish line. Offer:

   - Retainer or ongoing support packages

   - Advanced training or access

   - Group programs or masterminds

Let them know how they can continue with you.

5. **Referral and Loyalty Incentives**

Your best clients bring you more clients. Create a referral system or loyalty bonus for renewals and re-engagement to encourage repeat business.

Design a Retention-First Business

Start asking:

- How long can a client stay in my ecosystem?

- What services or products naturally follow the first offer?

- How am I tracking client success and satisfaction?

- Do I have a system for reactivation and follow-up?

When your business is retention-focused, you don't hustle as hard for revenue. You nurture it.

Metrics That Matter

Retention isn't a vibe. Track it.

Metric	Why It Matters
Client Retention %	How many clients return after a purchase
Customer Lifetime Value (CLTV)	Total revenue earned per client
Repeat Purchase Rate	Shows if clients buy again
Churn Rate	Tracks client drop-off or cancellations

You should also be familiar with these metrics, as well as your revenue.

Action Steps: Build a Retention Engine

1. Review your current onboarding experience and upgrade it.

2. Add one new touchpoint to your client experience this month.

3. Create a follow-up offer or next-level product.

4. Design a simple referral or loyalty program.

5. Track your retention rate and customer lifetime value (CLTV) on a quarterly basis.

Final Word: Don't Just Chase New — Nurture What You Have

You already did the hard work of earning the client's trust. Now, your job is to deepen it. You don't need more leads to grow. You need better *systems* to keep the ones you have.

Clients stay where they feel valued. Clients stay where results are real. Clients stay where CEOs *care*. So, keep them close and let your revenue rise with them.

Chapter 9
PAY YOURSELF LIKE A BOSS

◇

Credit & Acknowledgment

$\mathcal{S}$ome of the core financial philosophies referenced in this chapter—especially the practice of allocating income into designated accounts for profit, tax, and owner pay—are inspired by the Profit First methodology created by Mike Michalowicz. His book, *Profit First: Transform Your Business from a Cash-Eating Monster to a Money-Making Machine* (Portfolio/Penguin, 2014), has been a powerful resource in reshaping how entrepreneurs manage cash flow with intention. I encourage every business owner to read it and integrate its principles in alignment with their own strategy.

Owner's Compensation Strategy & Tax Planning for Real CEOs

If you're running a business and still struggling to pay yourself consistently, you don't have a profit problem; you have a *priority problem. You are the most important employee in your business.* And if your compensation is an afterthought, your business is not sustainable, no matter how good the revenue looks.

So many entrepreneurs brag about "six-figure launches" or big months, but they're still living check to check. Why? Because they've built a business that eats first and leaves them with scraps. Let's stop that now.

This chapter is about putting your pay at the top of the equation, not the bottom. It's about setting up your compensation like a true CEO and leveraging tax strategy so you can keep more of what you earn.

Stop Starving the Owner

If you're only paying yourself when "there's something left," you've built a fragile business model. It doesn't matter if you're making $20K/month. If you're not paying yourself intentionally and consistently, the business isn't profitable. It's just busy.

And busy doesn't build wealth. Here's your mindset shift:

Owner pay is not a reward. It's a requirement.

The Three (3) Ways Business Owners Get Paid

Your compensation depends on your business structure. But every structure must allow the owner to benefit fairly. Let's break it down:

1. **Salary (W-2)**
   - Required for S Corporations and C Corporations
   - Allows payroll taxes to be withheld properly
   - Useful for building retirement contributions, showing income for loans, and reducing audit risk

2. **Owner's Draw**
   - Common in sole proprietorships and LLCs
   - Money pulled directly from business equity
   - No taxes withheld — must plan quarterly

3. **Profit Distributions**
   - Paid out based on profits after operating expenses and salary
   - Not subject to self-employment tax (S Corps only)
   - Requires accurate bookkeeping and documentation

CPA Tip: If you're an S Corp owner, you need to pay yourself a *reasonable salary* — and then take additional profit distributions.

How Much Should You Pay Yourself?

There's no magic number. But there is an innovative formula.

Start by asking:

- What is the monthly minimum you need for personal living expenses?

- What does the business currently gross?

- What's the average net profit margin?

Profit-First Allocation (Example):

Category	% of Revenue
Owner Pay	40–50%
Operating Expenses	30–40%
Taxes	15%
Profit Reserve	5–10%

If your business grosses $10,000/month:

- Owner Pay = $4,000–$5,000

- Taxes = $1,500

- Profit = $500

- Ops = $3,000–$4,000

This is just a model. Adjust for your industry and stage. But the *principle* holds: *You come first.*

Create a Bankable Pay Structure

Set up your accounts and pay system:

Open three (3) business accounts:

- Operating

- Tax

- Profit

Automate transfers:

- Weekly or bi-weekly, based on revenue

- Use percentages, not feelings

Run payroll (if applicable):

- Use Gusto, ADP, QuickBooks Payroll or Surepayroll

- Set a regular pay schedule (monthly or biweekly)

Track your draws or distributions:

- Use a spreadsheet or accounting software

- Record payments clearly (Draw, Salary, Distribution)

Pay Yourself & Pay Less in Taxes

Here's where you get ahead: *Optimize your compensation to reduce tax liability.*

Tax-smart strategies include:

- Electing S Corp status to split income between salary and distribution

- Maximizing deductions (home office, vehicle, business travel, health insurance)*

- Contributing to Solo 401(k) or SEP IRA

- Leveraging the Augusta Rule (renting your home to your business for meetings, tax-free)

CPA Tip: Smart compensation = personal income + tax strategy + retirement growth. All three matter.

Monthly Compensation Check-In

Here's a simple monthly checklist to stay consistent:

Item	Done
Salary or draw paid on time.	
Profit transfer completed.	
Taxes are set aside.	
Owner Pay logged/tracked.	
Reviewed budget or KPIs.	

Make this your *non-negotiable Money Monday ritual.*

---

*Full Business Deductions list in SSBP workbook

Action Steps: Pay Yourself Like a Boss

1. Determine your ideal monthly owner pay.

2. Review current revenue and adjust pricing, if needed.

3. Set up or review banking and transfer structure.

4. Choose a payroll tool if incorporated.

5. Track compensation and evaluate quarterly.

Final Word: Pay First, Not Last

You didn't leave your job to work for free. You didn't build this thing to live paycheck to paycheck with a six-figure Stripe account. You're no longer an employee. You're the owner.

It's time to stop surviving in your business and start profiting from it. You earned this. So now? Pay yourself like a boss.

Chapter 10

SCALE INTELLIGENTLY, NOT IMPULSIVELY

◇

Know When, Why, and How to Grow Without Breaking Your Business

*L*et's get one thing straight. *Scaling is not just about getting bigger. It's about getting better.* Too many entrepreneurs rush to "scale" because they're chasing a feeling: more sales, more reach, more recognition. But if you scale a shaky business, all you do is grow the mess.

Scaling multiplies what already exists. So, if your systems are broken, your stress will be, too. Scaling should serve your *profit*, your *peace*, and your *purpose*. Not just your ego.

Let's break down how to scale with strategy, not stress.

What Does Scaling Actually Mean?

Scaling is increasing your revenue without increasing your chaos. It's building the capacity to serve more people *without* working more hours or hiring a bloated team. It means your business grows and *you can still live your life*.

Real scaling looks like this:

- More leads from the same effort

- Higher revenue from the same offer

- Increased delivery capacity without burning out

- Hiring with intention, not panic

- Automation replacing manual effort

If scaling feels like sprinting on a treadmill, you're doing it wrong.

Are You Ready to Scale?
Scaling Readiness Check

Is your core offer profitable and proven?	
Do you have documented systems and SOPs?	
Are you paying yourself consistently?	
Do you have the capacity to deliver more?	
Do you have at least three months of reserves?	

If more than two boxes are unchecked, pause. Build the foundation first.

The Most Common Scaling Mistakes
Let's call them out:

- Hiring a team before your systems are documented

- Launching a second offer before the first one is refined

- Taking on every opportunity instead of filtering based on alignment

- Scaling revenue while ignoring profit margins

- Building faster than your capacity to deliver

Scaling should feel like adding fuel to a well-tuned engine, not duct-taping the hood down.

Ways to Scale Without Losing Your Mind

Here are five sustainable scaling paths:

1. **Offer Optimization**
   - Raise prices to increase margin.

   - Create a product suite: Intro ⇨ Core ⇨ High ticket.

   - Add retainer or recurring models for predictable income.

2. Process Automation
   - Utilize tools such as Zapier, Dubsado, and ClickUp.

   - Automate onboarding, emails, and fulfillment.

   - Reduce manual hours.

3. Team Expansion (Intentionally)

    • Hire delivery help to expand capacity.

    • Bring in sales or marketing support.

    • Add project or operations management.

4. Licensing or Certification

    • Package your framework into a license.

    • Certify others to teach or deliver your method.

5. Digital or Passive Leverage

    • Courses, templates, paid communities

    • Systems that scale without 1:1 hours

Start with one. Nail it. Then grow.

Build a Scalable Infrastructure

Want to scale? Stop being the bottleneck.

Set up:

• A CRM for managing clients and leads

• A project management system (ClickUp, Trello)

• A fulfillment checklist for every offer

• Onboarding sequences for both clients and team

• Monthly dashboards for tracking KPIs

CPA Tip: Automate the repeatable. Delegate the teachable. Only you should do the visionary.

Action Steps: Scale Smart

- Audit your current capacity. What's already working well?

- Choose one scaling path to pursue over the next ninety days.

- Eliminate or simplify anything draining revenue or energy.

- Document your systems before you hire.

- Set revenue *and* profitability goals for scale. Don't grow broke.

Final Word: Don't Just Scale — Sustain

Growth is exciting. But sustainability is what keeps you in the game. Don't let speed seduce you into sabotage. You're not building fast. You're building *forever*.

Chapter 11
TURN PROFITS INTO PERMANENT WEALTH

---◇---

Use Your Business as the Engine for Legacy and Financial Freedom

*L*et me say something that many people won't: *Revenue is temporary. Wealth is permanent.* You didn't build this business just to make money. You built it to create options. To own your time. To protect your family. To leave something that outlasts you.

But that doesn't happen by accident. If you want your profits to mean something, you have to turn them into *assets*. This is where we stop chasing money and start building real wealth.

Why Most Entrepreneurs Stay Stuck

- They make money.

- They spend money.

- They reinvest money.

- And they never actually *keep* any money.

No one ever taught them how to move from income to independence. It's not enough to "pay yourself." You must learn how to *multiply yourself*.

The Five Wealth Buckets Every Founder Needs

Here's how I teach my clients to divide up their profit once the business is stable:

Bucket	Purpose
Emergency Fund	3–6 months of business + personal expenses
Tax Savings	Avoid IRS surprises — set aside monthly
Freedom Fund	Short-term security + peace of mind
Investment Account	Long-term wealth (stock market, real estate)
Legacy + Insurance	Life insurance, trust, estate planning

You don't have to fund all five today, but you do need a plan for each.

Set a Profit Transfer Plan

Don't just "hope to save." Automate your wealth. Here's a simple system:

- Pay yourself a base salary (consistent).

- Take monthly or quarterly profit distributions.

- Allocate percentages from that distribution.

Transfer	% Suggestion
Emergency Fund	20%
Investments	40%
Giving/Charity	10%
Retirement Savings	20
Fun or Celebration	10%

CPA Tip: Consult with your advisor about Solo 401(k)s, SEP IRAs, HSA accounts, and strategies for rental properties. These are power moves for business owners.

Protect the Wealth You're Building

Wealth isn't just about what you make. It's about what you protect. That includes:

- Solid business insurance

- LLC or corporate structures for asset protection

- Life insurance with the proper beneficiaries

- Estate planning (will, trust, power of attorney)

If you make money, but die without a plan, your wealth can be consumed by probate, taxes, or confusion. Build the castle *and* the moat.

Wealth Isn't a Flex — It's a Foundation

I don't want you just posting screenshots of Stripe payments. I want you:

- Getting approved for real estate deals

- Taking paid vacations without stress

- Retiring with dignity

- Leaving assets, not problems, for your children

Profit is just step one. Wealth is the *real* goal.

Action Steps: Build the Wealth Engine

1. Open a separate savings or brokerage account.

2. Set up an automated profit transfer %.

3. Meet with a financial advisor or planner.

4. Begin researching retirement and insurance options.

5. Update your legal documents for protection.

Final Word: Don't Just Make Money. Multiply It.

You didn't come this far to stay tired. You came to build freedom. Let your business fund your wealth. Let your profits serve your purpose. Let your legacy begin while you're still alive to enjoy it. This is the chapter where your business begins to work *for you*. Let's build real wealth. And never look back.

Conclusion
THE BANKABLE BUSINESS OWNER MINDSET

———◇———

Operating with Vision, Discipline, and Margin

*L*et's get one thing straight:

- You are not just a service provider.

- You are not just self-employed.

- You are not just "making it work."

You are the CEO of a business that banks profits. And that changes *everything*.

This book wasn't just about giving you steps. It was about *shifting your standards* and helping you finally run your business with clarity, confidence, and control. Because building a successful business isn't just about knowing what to do. It's about *who you become* while doing it.

And now? It's time to *operate*, not hustle. It's time to *lead*, not react. It's time to *build margin*, not just revenue. Let's break it down.

The Bankable Business Owner Operates with Vision

You don't get bankable results from random effort. You acquire them by running a business with purpose, strategy, and a long-term vision. You know:

- Who you serve and why

- What your most profitable offers are

- Where you're taking the company in one, three, and five years

- How your business funds your *life*, not the other way around

Vision isn't fluff. It's fuel. Without it, your business becomes a job with bad hours.

The Bankable Business Owner Leads with Discipline

Vision without discipline is just a dream. Discipline means:

- You check your numbers *before* you check Instagram.

- You hold your team accountable to KPIs.

- You set boundaries with clients, time, and money.

- You stop rescuing broken business models with more marketing.

You don't just "try harder". You implement systems. You don't chase motivation. You follow structure. You move with CEO energy every day, even when you don't feel like it.

The Bankable Business Owner Builds with Margin

Margin is the space between what you produce and what it costs you (financially, emotionally, physically).

Bankable businesses protect:

- Profit margin

- Time margin

- Energy margin

- Emotional margin

You stop saying, "Yes!" to every client. You charge what your offer is worth. You protect your time like a million-dollar asset because you are just that.

Your 12-Month SSBP Action Plan

This isn't the end — this is your execution season.

Let's turn all of this knowledge into real momentum.

Quarter 1: Foundation + Pricing

- Refine your offers for profitability.

- Register or restructure your entity, if needed.

- Implement your back office systems.

- Run a pricing audit and set new price points.

- Start paying yourself consistently.

Quarter 2: Operations + Team

- Document your SOPs.

- Hire your first or next profit-aligned team member.

- Establish KPIs and reporting rhythms.

- Improve delivery and client experience systems.

- Start tracking retention and client lifetime value.

Quarter 3: Scale + Automate

- Choose your primary scaling strategy (team, digital, licensing).

- Automate onboarding, emails, and financial reports.

- Begin exit-planning or succession documentation.

- Create or refine a recurring revenue model.

- Set monthly revenue and profit margin goals.

Quarter 4: Wealth + Legacy

- Set personal financial goals and wealth buckets.

- Meet with a financial advisor and/or estate planner.

- Automate business-to-personal profit transfers.

- Invest in retirement, insurance, and legal protections to secure your financial future.

- Plan your CEO retreat or recharge quarter.

Final Charge: You Are the Asset

This entire book—every chapter, every checklist, every mindset shift—was about *reclaiming your power* as a business owner. You are not building this to burn out. You are not here to scrape by. You were called to build something that sustains you, funds your freedom, and leaves a legacy.

No more small thinking. No more hiding behind imposter syndrome. No more broken business models.

You are *bankable*. Now, go run your business like it. Thank you for allowing me to pour into your life and business.

Bonus Chapter

PERSONAL FINANCIAL HEALTH FOR BUSINESS OWNERS

◇

Personal Money Systems Every Business Owner Needs to Build Wealth with Peace

*Y*ou're running the business. You're making money. You've got clients, content, contracts. But your *personal finances?* They are a little shaky.

Let me be clear. I've worked with high-income founders who were great at running their businesses. However, behind the scenes, their credit was in disrepair, their savings were nonexistent, and they were quietly scared to open their personal banking app. Sound familiar?

Here's the truth: *Your business can only grow as far as your personal financial foundation can support it.* This chapter is about tightening up your *household money* the way you've tightened up your business. Because your next level of peace and profit starts at *home.*

Why Founders Neglect Their Personal Finances

You're too busy building. You think business income will "cover everything." You've adopted a wait-until-I-make-more approach. You think you can't budget because your income is inconsistent.

Let me tell you something: *Making more money does not fix messy money*. You need structure. If you want financial independence, early retirement, and wealth you can pass down, you must treat your personal money like a CEO, not a crisis manager.

Step 1: Know Your Personal Financial Baseline

You cannot improve what you don't measure. Start with these.

Metric	Why It Matters
Credit Score	Impacts lending, insurance, and homeownership
Net Worth (Assets – Debts)	Snapshot of your actual wealth
Monthly Cash Flow	Are you living within your means?
Emergency Savings	Security when business slows, or emergencies hit

- Get a personal finance tracker.

- Check your credit report (free at
  AnnualCreditReport.com).

- List your current savings, debts, and recurring expenses.

Step 2: Pay Yourself the Right Way

We covered this in Chapter 9, but here's a personal twist. When your business pays you, that money becomes *your household income.* What you do with it *after that* matters just as much.

Create a personal "paycheck" process:

- If required to have a payroll, determine a reasonable wage,

- If LLC or Sole Proprietor, transfer a fixed amount to your personal account (weekly or bi-weekly)

- Treat it like a W-2 paycheck — not a random draw

- Use a budgeting app such as YNAB, EveryDollar, or Monarch to give every dollar a purpose.

This consistency makes it easier to qualify for home loans, credit, or future funding.

Step 3: Build a Personal Spending Plan (Not a Restrictive Budget)

Your business has structure — your personal life needs it too. Use this simple framework:

Bucket	% Recommendation
Essentials	50% (housing, food, utilities)
Financial Growth	20% (savings, debt payoff, investing)
Freedom + Joy	20% (travel, dining, hobbies)
Giving	10% (charity, family, faith)

This is a guide — not a prison. The point is to *intentionally assign* your money to your values and goals.

Step 4: Automate Your Wealth

Wealth doesn't grow by accident. Set up automation to do the heavy lifting:

- Direct deposit from business to personal account

- Automatic transfers to savings, investment, and tax accounts

- Auto-pay for bills and minimum debts

- Quarterly financial review with your CPA or advisor

Your goal is to make wealth-building effortless.

Step 5: Protect the Asset — You

You are your #1 asset. If you're not protected, neither is your business. Make sure you have:

- **Health insurance** (even if it's a high-deductible plan)

- **Life insurance** (term life is affordable and smart)

- **Disability insurance** (what happens if you can't work?)

- **Retirement account** (Solo 401(k), SEP IRA, Roth IRA)

- **Estate** plan (will, power of attorney, healthcare directive)

If you don't have a plan for your money, the IRS, creditors, or probate court will make one for you.

Build a Personal Financial Freedom Timeline

Let's flip the script. Instead of asking, "Can I afford this now?" Instead, ask:

- What does my ideal lifestyle cost monthly?

- How much money do I want to save or invest by the time I'm 40, 50, or 60?

- When do I want to retire — and what does that look like?

- What steps do I need to take each quarter to achieve this goal?

Now, reverse-engineer your strategy.

Action Steps: Founder Financial Fitness Plan

1. Pull your latest credit report and score.

2. Create a personal budget or spending plan for this month.

3. Automate transfers to at least one savings account.

4. Schedule a quarterly "wealth review" day.

5. Open a retirement or brokerage account (if you haven't already).

Final Word: You Deserve Peace in Your Personal Life, Too

It's time to stop using your business as a means to escape financial fear. Use your business to fund financial freedom. Use your business to protect your legacy. Use your business to give your future self options.

Don't build a profitable business and stay personally broke. You're too smart. Too powerful. Too gifted for that. Let's get financially fit — and stay that way.

SSBP BOOK REFERENCES

◇

- Michalowicz, M. (2014). *Profit First: Transform your business from a cash-eating monster to a money-making machine.* Portfolio/Penguin.

- Gerber, M. E. (2004). *The E-Myth Revisited: Why most small businesses don't work and what to do about it.* Harper Business.

- Guillebeau, C. (2012). *The $100 Startup: Reinvent the way you make a living, do what you love, and create a new future.* Crown Business.

- Vaynerchuk, G. (2018). *Crushing It!: How great entrepreneurs build their business and influence—and how you can, too.* HarperBusiness.

- Kiyosaki, R. T. (2000). *Rich Dad's Guide to Investing: What the rich invest in, that the poor and the middle class do not!.* Warner Books.

TOOLS & FINANCIAL CONCEPTS

◇

- IRS. (2023). *Understanding S Corporations*. Retrieved from https://www.irs.gov/businesses/small-businesses-self-employed/s-corporations

- QuickBooks. (n.d.). *Small business accounting software*. Retrieved from https://quickbooks.intuit.com/

- Gusto. (n.d.). *Payroll, benefits, and HR software for small businesses*. Retrieved from https://gusto.com/

- ClickUp. (n.d.). *All-in-one productivity platform*. Retrieved from https://clickup.com/

- U.S. Small Business Administration. (n.d.). *Write your business plan*. Retrieved from https://www.sba.gov/business-guide/plan-your-business/write-your-business-plan

FINANCIAL WELLNESS & PERSONAL WEALTH TOOLS

◇

- AnnualCreditReport.com. (n.d.). *Free credit reports.* Retrieved from https://www.annualcreditreport.com/

- YNAB – You Need A Budget. (n.d.). *Budgeting software and education.* Retrieved from https://www.youneedabudget.com/

- NerdWallet. (n.d.). *Compare financial products and tools.* Retrieved from https://www.nerdwallet.com/

- Investopedia. (n.d.). *Financial education and investment resources.* Retrieved from https://www.investopedia.com/

ABOUT THE AUTHOR

———————◇———————

*F*or more than 30 years, she has helped six-figure CEOs go from bankruptcy and broke to millionaires with the right systems and strategies. While many financial experts teach theory, Nicole Gillyard, CPA, speaker and coach teaches transformation—allowing her clientele to experience, lasting results. When it comes to problem solving with precision, The Profit-ista, as Nicole is affectionately known, is all about the numbers. Educating and empowering businesses and companies of all sizes to operate efficiently, yield a profit, and see bankable results, she understands how essential it is to know your numbers and interpret the hard truths they reveal about your business.

As the CEO and founder of By The Numberz CPA™, Nicole strives to help businesses reach an optimal level of operation as they scale and grow. Recognizing that too many small business owners work tirelessly, yet leave profits on the table, she strategically helps them to lay a firm foundation for their business and achieve stability before they scale. Noted as one of the Top 50 Women In Accounting by *ignition,* Nicole helps business owners who underprice their services, have inconsistent cash flow, and get unwanted tax surprises to build a business they not only love—but one that pays them consistently well.

Featured in the *Atlanta Daily World, The Atlanta Journal-Constitution* and *Madame Noire,* to name a few, Nicole is honored to be a monthly financial contributor for *Signature Bride.* Holding both an MBA and a BBA in Accounting from Eastern Michigan University, she is licensed as a CPA. In her debut book, *Start, Stay & Bank Profits™, The High-Income Entrepreneur's Guide to Building a Sustainable Business that Pays You for Life,* CPA and financial expert Nicole Gillyard offers a step-by-step guide for high-performing entrepreneurs and consultants to turn income into wealth, hustle into systems, and confusion into clarity.

A member of the American Institute of Certified Public Accountants and Certified Fraud Examiners, Nicole is a highly sought after speaker who hosts multiple masterclasses and workshops for business owners virtually and throughout Georgia. She plans to test for her CFE certification in the near future. By the beginning of 2026, By The Numberz will expand to include the C-Park Business Hub, a dynamic co-working and affordable office lease space located in College Park, Georgia. There, Nicole will offer her signature course, Start, Stay and Bank Profits, programs and workshops for business owners at every stage.

For booking or speaking engagements, email nkirkland@bythenumberzcpa.com.